VEGETARIAN GOURMET

COLE GROUP

© 1995 Cole Group, Inc.

Front cover photograph: Keith Ovregaard

Cole Group and Cole's Cooking Companion are trademarks of CHI/Cole Holdings, Inc.

Cole Group
1330 N. Dutton Ave., Suite 103
Santa Rosa, CA 95401
(800) 959-2717   (707) 526-2682
Fax (707) 526-2687

Printed in Hong Kong

G F E D C B A
1 0 9 8 7 6 5

ISBN 1-56426-807-1

Library of Congress Catalog Card Number in process

Distributed to the book trade by Publishers Group West

CONTENTS

A GOURMET APPROACH TO VEGETARIAN CUISINE

*W*ith lighter, more nutritious foods becoming a priority for good health, more and more people are taking a closer look at the vegetarian approach to cooking and eating. But, as you'll discover in *Vegetarian Gourmet,* health concerns are only part of the reason this type of cuisine is commanding increased attention.

A RATIONALE FOR VEGETARIAN COOKING

From a nutritional standpoint, grains, beans and peas, and fresh produce are ideal fuels for the human body. Abundant in complex carbohydrates (which most nutritionists consider a superior source of energy) they are also higher in fiber, vitamins, and minerals and lower in fat than most food products from animal sources. Nutritional advantages aside, these same foods can easily be transformed into an immense variety of economical vegetarian dishes with unique culinary appeal.

THE VEGETARIAN PANTRY

Becoming a gourmet vegetarian cook doesn't require retrofitting your kitchen, but you will need to stock up on some basic supplies. The goal is to ensure that you always have on hand the staples and other ingredients that complement the fresh foods each season and locale has to offer. The foods described in this section are featured in recipes in *Vegetarian Gourmet;* most of them are relatively inexpensive and all are widely available in supermarkets, natural food stores, and specialty markets.

Grains and Flours Their nutritive value and the breadth of their culinary uses make cereal grains the earth's most significant cultivated crop. *Rice* is the single most important food grown, sustaining more than half the world's population. *Brown rice* contains both the bran (the nutrient-rich outer coating of the grain) and the germ (the portion of the kernel containing other important nutrients). Only the tough outer hull is removed from brown rice during processing, whereas both the bran and most of the germ are removed to produce *white rice*. Long-grain varieties are dry and fluffy when cooked, while short-grain and medium-grain varieties develop a creamy, sticky texture. *Wild rice*, prized

---

The nutritional and dietary information and suggestions in this book are presented as topics of general interest and are not intended to replace the recommendations of a qualified health professional. Because individuals vary in their nutritional needs, you should consult with a qualified health professional before making any major modifications in the diets of adults or children.

for its nutty flavor and earthy fragrance, is actually not a variety of rice at all but the seed of an aquatic grass.

Wheat is second only to rice in its significance worldwide. *Whole wheat flour* retains the bran and germ of the whole grain. Processing removes both the bran and germ from *unbleached wheat flour,* although, unlike all-purpose flour, it is not chemically whitened. *Couscous* is a precooked wheat product made from semolina, a high-protein variety of wheat used for *pasta. Corn* in the form of tortillas and other masa-based dishes is the foundation of cooking in Mexico; in northern Italy, coarsely ground cornmeal known as *polenta* is a staple. *Buckwheat groats, flour,* and *kasha* (the Russian name for toasted buckwheat groats or grits) have a full-bodied flavor that complements many vegetables. Any grains and flours you purchase should come from a reputable source with a rapid turnover of stock. At home, store grain products in airtight containers in a cool, dry place or under refrigeration.

Legumes The high food value of dried beans and peas and their satisfying taste make them popular the world over. Properly combined with grains, nuts, and seeds, they provide more nutritional value than beef, cheese, fish, or poultry. Legumes that are eaten fresh, before they mature, include *green beans, shelled fresh peas,* and *snow peas.* Dried legumes include *chick-peas* (garbanzos), *lentils, lima beans, navy beans, pinto beans,* and *soybeans*—used fresh or dried, processed into *tofu,* or fermented and aged to make condiments such as *soy sauce, tamari,* and *miso.* Fresh beans and peas should be treated like any other perishable produce. Dried legumes will keep well for up to a year if they are properly stored in airtight containers in a cool, dry place. When preparing dried beans and peas for cooking, look them over carefully and remove any stones, debris, and broken or split pieces. Clean them before cooking by rinsing them several times; soak overnight to soften them before cooking. To avoid an unpleasant appearance and taste in cooked legumes, skim off any gray foam that forms as they first begin to boil. Because salting the cooking liquid tends to toughen legumes, wait to season them until they are fully cooked.

Fruits and Vegetables More than any other ingredient used in vegetarian cooking, fruits and vegetables contribute the variety and freshness that are the essence of all great cuisines. The diversity of fresh produce available in the market reflects the increasing interest in the nutritional advantages of fresh fruits and vegetables, as well as curiosity about the fresh foods and other ingredients used in the cuisines of other cultures. Buying produce when the harvest is at its peak is the most economical way to enjoy it while ensuring that the fruits and vegetables will have the very best flavor. Be sure the fruits and vegetables you select are free of moldy spots or bruises and pleasing to the eye, nose, and palate. Use fresh produce as soon as possible after harvesting or purchasing it, before it loses nutrients and flavor.

Nuts and Seeds Nuts and seeds are high in nutrients, including unsaturated fats (see below), and contribute a satisfying taste and texture to vegetarian cooking. Because they are highly perishable, plan to purchase only as much as you can use in a relatively short time. Store them in airtight containers in a cool, dry place (or in the refrigerator or freezer) and discard any that develop a rancid odor or taste.

Fats and Oils Fats and oils carry the flavor and aroma of foods, adding a satisfying richness to a wide range of dishes. But, depending on their molecular structure, some fats are better for you than others. Nutritionists everywhere are urging a reduction in the consumption of saturated fats—the type in animal products, including dairy foods, and in vegetable products such as shortening, margarine, chocolate, and coconut and palm oils. Unsaturated fats are considered healthier from a nutritional standpoint and are found in nuts and seeds, and in canola, corn, olive, safflower, and other vegetable oils, as well as fish and chicken. Most nutritional experts agree that a balanced diet for adults should contain no more than 30 percent fat; ideally, saturated fats should make up no more than 10 percent of the total intake of calories.

Oils are highly perishable and should be purchased in small quantities, stored in a cool, dark place, and used within eight weeks or less. Heating certain unsaturated oils to the smoking

point can cause them to break down and become saturated. In selecting oil for a recipe, choose one with a flavor and aroma and cooking characteristics that complement the food being prepared: for example, virgin olive oil for salads and for drizzling over cooked dishes; Asian sesame oil for stir-frying and Asian dishes; corn oil and other mild-flavored oils for baking.

DEFINING "VEGETARIAN"

The *Vegetarian Gourmet* includes dishes for three general categories of vegetarian diets: The most restricted is a *vegan* diet, limited to only grains, legumes, nuts and seeds, fruits, and vegetables. For most people dairy products are an important source of nutrients, including the vitamin B^{12} needed for proper cell development and functioning of the nervous system. Because milk products are not a part of a vegan diet, other sources of Vitamin B^{12} (such as miso and other fermented soy products, nutritional yeast, or dietary supplements) should be included. A *lacto-vegetarian* approach includes dairy products in a varied vegetarian diet, while an *ovo-lacto-vegetarian* diet includes both eggs and dairy products. The diets of most vegetarians fall into one of these categories; however, for many other people, an occasional serving of meat, poultry, or fish is not incompatible with a balanced approach to vegetarian cooking and eating.

RECIPES AND TECHNIQUES FOR VEGETARIAN COOKING

Mastering vegetarian cooking is a
matter of using a few basic techniques to
imaginatively combine grains, legumes, and
other nutritious staples with the fresh produce
each season has to offer. From soups, salads,
and other meal-time starters and light meals to
main dishes, accompaniments, and desserts,
this collection of more than 50 gourmet recipes
showcases the remarkable versatility, economy,
and appeal of vegetarian cooking.

STARTERS AND LIGHT MEALS

An engaging assortment of delightful soups, salads and other mealtime openers that can double as light entrées is a worthwhile addition to any cook's repertoire. From Andalusian Gazpacho to Spinach-Cheese Roulade, Deep-Fried Zucchini Blossoms, and Vegetarian Potstickers, the recipes in this section point up the variety and versatility of vegetarian cooking.

Soup au Pistou

This French soup with a pesto topping depends on fresh vegetables and herbs for its unusually fine flavor and visual appeal.

12 cups	Vegetarian Stock (see page 16)	2.7 l
½ cup	cooked navy beans	125 ml
1	onion, diced	1
1	leek, cleaned and thinly sliced	1
¼ cup	chopped celery with leaves	60 ml
½ cup	diced red new potato	125 ml
1 tsp	olive oil	1 tsp
2	carrots, diced	2
1	tomato, peeled, seeded, and chopped	1
½ cup	sliced green beans	125 ml
½ cup	sliced zucchini	125 ml
½ cup	penne or macaroni	125 ml
½ tsp	freshly ground black pepper	½ tsp
to taste	salt	to taste

Pistou

2 cloves	garlic, minced	2 cloves
1 cup	chopped fresh basil leaves	250 ml
½ cup	freshly grated Parmesan cheese	125 ml

1. In a large pot bring stock to a boil. Add navy beans, onion, leek, celery, potato, oil, carrots, tomato, green beans, zucchini, and pasta. Simmer until vegetables and pasta are tender (about 30–40 minutes). Remove from heat and add pepper and salt to taste.

2. To prepare Pistou, in a blender or food processor, combine garlic, basil, and cheese. Blend to a smooth purée.

3. Ladle soup into large bowls and garnish each serving with 2–3 teaspoons Pistou. Pass extra Pistou at table, if desired.

Makes 6 servings.

WILD RICE AND MUSHROOM SOUP

This earthy soup uses both fresh and dried mushrooms. Serve it with whole-grain bread or muffins as the first course of a hearty winter meal.

½ cup	dried porcini or shiitake mushrooms	125 ml
4 cups	Vegetarian Stock (see page 16)	900 ml
1½ cups	sliced fresh button mushrooms	350 ml
½	onion, chopped	½
⅓ cup	wild rice, rinsed	85 ml
to taste	salt and freshly ground black pepper	to taste
as needed	sour cream or yogurt	as needed
as needed	chopped parsley, for garnish	as needed

1. Cover dried mushrooms with hot water and set aside while preparing other ingredients.

2. In a large saucepan combine stock, fresh mushrooms, onion, and wild rice. Bring to a boil. Reduce heat and simmer, uncovered.

3. Remove dried mushrooms from soaking liquid, reserving liquid. Add mushrooms to soup. Strain soaking liquid through cheesecloth and add to saucepan. Continue cooking until wild rice is tender (35–45 minutes). Season to taste with salt and pepper.

4. Ladle soup into individual bowls. Add a spoonful of sour cream or yogurt to each and sprinkle with parsley for garnish.

Serves 4 to 6.

Vegetarian Stock

This economical soup base adds flavor and body to soups, stews, and other dishes.

3 tbl	butter	3 tbl
2	leeks	2
3	carrots, chopped	3
3 stalks	celery, with leaves, thinly sliced	3 stalks
2	onions, chopped	2
1 clove	garlic, slivered	1 clove
12 cups	water	2.7 l
2 tsp	salt	2 tsp
5 sprigs	Italian (flat-leaf) parsley, with stems	5 sprigs
1	bay leaf	1
1 tsp	dried thyme	1 tsp
¼ tsp	coarsely cracked black peppercorns	¼ tsp

1. In a large kettle over medium heat, melt butter. Add leeks, carrots, celery, onions, and garlic; cook, stirring often, until vegetables are soft but not browned (15–20 minutes).

2. Add the water, salt, parsley, bay leaf, thyme, and peppercorns. Bring slowly to a boil. Then cover, reduce heat, and simmer for 2 hours.

3. Strain stock, discarding vegetables and any solids. Let the stock cool, then cover and refrigerate. Use within 3–4 days or freeze for up to 2 weeks.

Makes about 10 cups (2.3 l).

NORTHERN CHINESE HOT AND SOUR SOUP

One of the most popular items in Chinese restaurants, this peppery soup originally was created as a traditional medicinal preparation. Look for the bamboo shoots, dried black and cloud ear mushrooms, and dried lily buds at Asian markets or natural food stores.

4 cups	Vegetarian Stock (see page 16)	900 ml
6 slices	fresh ginger	6 slices
¼ cup each	shredded carrots and Chinese cabbage	60 ml each
¼ cup	sliced green onion	60 ml
¼ cup	sliced bamboo shoots	60 ml
2 large	black mushrooms, soaked, drained, stems removed, and sliced	2 large
¼ cup each	cloud ear mushrooms and lily buds, soaked and drained	60 ml each
1 cake (7 oz)	firm tofu, pressed and diced (see page 63)	1 cake (200 g)
2 tbl	rice vinegar, or to taste	2 tbl
3 tbl	soy sauce	3 tbl
¼ tsp	freshly ground black pepper	¼ tsp
1 tbl	cornstarch	1 tbl
to taste	salt and freshly ground black pepper	to taste
½ cup	fresh peas, blanched	125 ml
2	eggs, lightly beaten	2

1. Bring stock to a boil with ginger slices. Discard ginger. Add carrots, cabbage, green onions, bamboo shoots, black and cloud ear mushrooms, lily buds, and tofu; simmer until vegetables are just tender, about 4 minutes.

2. In a small bowl combine vinegar, soy sauce, pepper, and cornstarch; stir to dissolve cornstarch. Add to soup and cook until raw starch flavor disappears (about 2 minutes). Adjust seasoning, if necessary, with salt, pepper, or additional rice vinegar. Add blanched peas. Pour eggs over surface of soup; allow to set for a few seconds. Stir to make "egg flowers." Serve immediately.

Serves 4.

CURRIED ACORN SQUASH BISQUE

This lowfat bisque has a robust flavor that surpasses anything made with packaged curry powders.

2	acorn squash	2
1 tsp	olive oil	1 tsp
½ cup	minced onion	125 ml
2 cloves	garlic, minced	2 cloves
1	red bell pepper, seeded and finely diced	1
⅓ cup	dry sherry	85 ml
2½ cups	Vegetarian Stock (see page 16)	600 ml
1 cup	freshly squeezed orange juice	250 ml
½ tsp	ground cumin	½ tsp
½ tsp	ground coriander	½ tsp
1 tsp	grated fresh ginger	1 tsp
¼ tsp	dry mustard	¼ tsp
to taste	salt	to taste
¼ tsp	cayenne pepper	¼ tsp
¼ tsp	white pepper	¼ tsp
¼ cup	nonfat yogurt	60 ml

1. Preheat oven to 350°F (175°C). Split squash lengthwise, leaving in the seeds. Place halves, split side down, on a baking sheet. Bake until soft (about 40 minutes).

2. Scoop out squash seeds and discard. Scoop flesh from shells and mash well; set aside. Discard shells.

3. In a large stockpot, heat oil; add onion and sauté over medium heat until onion is soft. Add garlic, bell pepper, and sherry; cook 5 minutes. Add remaining ingredients except yogurt.

4. Bring to a boil, lower heat, cover, and simmer for 35 minutes. Remove from heat, purée in blender or food processor and stir in yogurt. Taste for seasoning and serve hot.

Serves 4.

ANDALUSIAN GAZPACHO

From the Spanish plains comes a refreshingly crisp, chilled salad-in-a-soup that is perfect on a hot summer day; the ingredients are blended but not cooked.

1	cucumber, peeled, seeded, and diced	1
1	green bell pepper, seeded and diced	1
5	green onions, chopped	5
2 cloves	garlic, minced	2 cloves
3	tomatoes, diced	3
2 stalks	celery, diced	2 stalks
1	avocado, peeled, seeded, and diced	1
⅓ cup	minced parsley	85 ml
⅓ cup	minced fresh basil	85 ml
1 tbl	minced fresh oregano	1 tbl
2½ cups	navy beans, cooked	600 ml
2 tbl	olive oil	2 tbl
6 tbl	red wine vinegar	6 tbl
2 tsp	salt	2 tsp
1 tsp	ground cumin	1 tsp
1 can (46 oz)	tomato juice	1 can (1.35 kg)
	or	
5½ cups	Vegetarian Stock (see page 16)	1.2 l

1. Place all ingredients in a 4-quart (3.6-l) soup tureen. Stir to mix thoroughly and chill 4–12 hours.

2. Serve in chilled soup bowls.

Serves 10.

PILAF SALAD

This satisfying vegetarian salad can be baked or simmered on top of the stove for 20 minutes before being tossed with a vinaigrette dressing.

2½ cups	Vegetarian Stock (see page 16)	600 ml
½ cup	raisins	125 ml
1½ tbl	butter	1½ tbl
1½ tbl	olive oil	1½ tbl
½	onion, diced	½
¾ cup	long-grain rice (see page 6)	175 ml
½ cup	dried lentils	125 ml
⅛ tsp each	ground cardamom, ground cinnamon, ground cloves, ground coriander, ground cumin, and freshly ground black pepper	⅛ tsp each
1½ cups	sliced green beans	350 ml
1	potato, diced	1
½ cup	fresh or frozen petits pois (tiny peas)	125 ml
1 cup	diced carrot	250 ml
½ cup	diced red or green bell pepper	125 ml
as needed	chopped cilantro (coriander leaves)	as needed

1. Preheat oven to 375°F (175°C). In large saucepan over medium heat, combine stock and raisins and bring to a boil. Remove from heat and keep warm.

2. In large ovenproof skillet over medium-high heat, melt butter and oil. Add onions and sauté until lightly browned.

3. Stir in rice, lentils, cardamom, cinnamon, cloves, coriander, cumin, and pepper. Stir and cook 2–3 minutes. Add green beans, potato, peas, carrot, and bell pepper; pour in stock and raisins.

4. Cover and bake until all liquid has been absorbed (about 20 minutes). Remove from oven, sprinkle with chopped cilantro, and serve hot.

Serves 5 to 6.

DEEP-FRIED ZUCCHINI BLOSSOMS

Be sure to use only unsprayed blossoms for this recipe.

Batter

2	eggs, separated	2
½ cup	water	125 ml
¼ cup	white wine	60 ml
2 tbl	olive oil	2 tbl
1 tsp	Worcestershire sauce	1 tsp
1 cup	unbleached flour	250 ml
½ tsp	salt	½ tsp
2 cups	grated mozzarella cheese	500 ml
2	fresh jalapeño chiles, chopped	2
30	squash blossoms, stems removed	30
as needed	oil, for frying	as needed
as needed	salt and freshly ground black pepper	as needed

1. To prepare the batter, in a blender combine all the batter ingredients (reserving egg whites) and process on high speed. Let batter stand at least 1 hour.

2. In a medium bowl toss together mozzarella and chopped chiles. Gently stuff blossoms with cheese mixture, twisting ends of blossoms to seal.

3. Beat reserved egg whites to soft peaks; fold into batter. In a deep skillet heat 3–4 inches (7.5–10 cm) of oil to 370°F (185°C). Dip blossoms one by one into batter, making sure they are completely coated. Drop into hot oil, frying several at once and turning occasionally. When blossoms are a golden color, remove from pan with a slotted spoon and drain on paper towels. Sprinkle with salt and pepper; serve hot.

Makes 30 appetizers.

UDON SALAD

Udon noodles are a favorite of Japanese cuisine. Both the noodles and Asian sesame oil can be found in most natural food stores or Asian markets.

12 oz	cooked udon noodles (see below)	350 g
2 tbl	grated fresh ginger	2 tbl
5 oz	sliced water chestnuts	140 g
2 cups	sliced mushrooms	500 ml
2 tbl	chopped peanuts	2 tbl
¼ cup	Asian sesame oil	60 ml
5 cloves	garlic, minced	5 cloves
6	green onions, minced	6
1–2 tsp	cayenne pepper	1–2 tsp
½ cup	soy sauce or tamari	125 ml
½ tsp	honey	½ tsp
as needed	lettuce leaves	as needed

1. Place noodles in a bowl. Mix together remaining ingredients except lettuce and toss with noodles.

2. Let marinate for 45 minutes before serving. Serve in a lettuce-lined bowl.

Serves 8.

COOKING UDON NOODLES

These delicate wheat noodles make a satisfying light meal or snack. Place the noodles in a large pot of lightly salted, rapidly boiling stock or water and stir to separate the noodles. Test for doneness a couple of minutes after the water returns to a boil. Precise cooking times vary from one brand of packaged noodle to another. As soon as the noodles are done to taste, drain them in a colander and serve. To store the cooked noodles several hours or overnight, rinse them with cold water until they are thoroughly cooled. Drain well, toss with a little Asian sesame oil, and store tightly wrapped in the refrigerator.

CHILLED JAPANESE NOODLES

Icy-cold noodles tossed with a soy sauce-sesame oil dressing and served with a colorful array of crisp vegetables and other toppings are perfect for warm-weather meals.

1 lb	cooked udon noodles (see page 27)	450 g
2 tbl	peanut oil	2 tbl

Noodle Dressing

3 tbl	soy sauce or tamari	3 tbl
3 tbl	Asian sesame oil	3 tbl
4 tsp	rice vinegar	4 tsp
1 tbl	sugar	1 tbl
½–1½ tsp	chile oil	½–1½ tsp
1 tsp	finely minced fresh ginger	1 tsp

as needed	carrots, finely grated	as needed
	cucumber, sliced paper-thin	
	green onions, minced	
	snow peas or green beans, blanched and sliced	
	fresh bean sprouts	
	fresh cilantro (coriander leaves), chopped	
	celery, sliced diagonally	
	peanuts or cashews, toasted and chopped	
	sesame seed, toasted	

1. Toss cooked noodles with peanut oil and set aside.

2. To prepare dressing, combine all ingredients in a bowl large enough to hold noodles; stir to dissolve sugar. Add noodles to bowl containing dressing and toss to coat evenly. Set aside at room temperature or in refrigerator until ready to serve, preferably overnight.

3. Prepare toppings. Toss noodles just before serving and serve in individual bowls. Arrange toppings on a serving platter.

Serves 4.

PASTA SALAD WITH CHICK-PEAS

Make this salad up to three days in advance—it gets better as it sits. For a quick lunch, drain some of the vinaigrette and stuff the salad into pita bread.

1½ cups	cooked chick-peas	350 ml
2 cups	cooked and drained shell pasta	500 ml
¾ cup	apple cider vinegar	175 ml
2 tbl	olive oil	2 tbl
1 tbl	safflower oil	1 tbl
⅓ cup	minced parsley	85 ml
⅓ cup	diced red bell pepper	85 ml
¼ cup	minced fresh dill	60 ml
dash	ground cumin	dash
as needed	salt and freshly ground black pepper	as needed
as needed	lettuce	as needed

1. Combine all ingredients except lettuce and chill 2 hours, stirring thoroughly at least twice.

2. Serve chilled on a bed of lettuce or use as a sandwich filling.

Serves 6.

COOKING PASTA

To cook pasta properly requires about 1 quart (900 ml) rapidly boiling water to every 2 cups (500 ml) of pasta. Salting the water adds flavor but is not essential.

- *Cook dried lasagne for 8–10 minutes, shells for 7–8 minutes, and fine pasta such as angel hair for 5–7 minutes, or until al dente. Fresh pasta needs only 2 minutes or less.*

- *Drain the cooked pasta and toss it with sauce or other ingredients right away. If the sauce needs thinning, use a bit of the cooking water.*

BEAN SALAD DIJON

This delicate but satisfying salad is a fine complement to Spinach-Cheese Roulade (see recipe and photo on pages 32–33). Steam the green beans just until their color intensifies and then immediately toss them with the marinade to keep the color bright. Depending on the size of the beans, you can either leave them whole or slice them diagonally into bite-sized pieces. This salad will keep well for three to four days, if covered and refrigerated.

1 lb	green beans, steamed lightly	450 g
1 cup	cooked navy beans	250 ml
1	lemon, juiced	1
2 oz	toasted, slivered almonds	60 g
1 tbl	chopped parsley	1 tbl
¼ cup	diced red bell pepper	60 ml
¼ cup	olive oil	60 ml
⅓ cup	rice vinegar	85 ml
2 tbl	Dijon mustard	2 tbl
as needed	lettuce leaves, for bowl	as needed

1. Combine all ingredients except lettuce and toss well to coat beans thoroughly.

2. Let marinate at room temperature for 45 minutes. Arrange in lettuce-lined bowl and serve.

Serves 4 to 6.

SPINACH-CHEESE ROULADE

This scrumptious entrée features a layered spinach mixture with a soufflé-like texture.

⅓ cup	finely minced onion	85 ml
1 tsp	olive oil	1 tsp
3 cups	chopped spinach leaves	700 ml
⅓ cup	finely minced parsley	85 ml
¼ cup	grated mozzarella cheese	60 ml
6	eggs, separated	6
as needed	oil, for parchment	as needed
2 cups	farmer or ricotta cheese	500 ml
2 tbl	freshly grated Parmesan cheese	2 tbl

1. Preheat oven to 400°F (205°C). In a skillet over medium-high heat, sauté onion in olive oil until very soft. Add spinach and parsley and cover. Cook over low heat for 2 minutes. Drain if excess liquid accumulates.

2. Transfer to a bowl. Stir mozzarella cheese and egg yolks into spinach mixture.

3. Cut a piece of parchment paper to fit into a shallow baking dish; lightly oil the parchment.

4. In a separate bowl beat egg whites until soft peaks form and fold them into spinach mixture. Spoon into the parchment-lined baking dish. Cover with another piece of lightly oiled parchment. Bake for 25 minutes.

5. In a bowl mix farmer and Parmesan cheeses and set aside. When soufflé is baked, flip it out of the baking dish onto the countertop. Peel off the top sheet of parchment and spread the cheese mixture over the soufflé.

6. Roll soufflé and cheese mixture as you would a jelly roll, peeling off the second sheet of parchment as you go. Cut into 6 slices and serve.

Serves 6.

STUFFED CHILES

A favorite appetizer or light luncheon dish from the American Southwest, this recipe calls for fresh chiles, but you can substitute canned chiles or bell peppers if necessary.

12	fresh Anaheim chiles	12
1 tsp	oil, for baking dish	1 tsp
¼ cup	dry sherry	60 ml
1 tsp	olive oil	1 tsp
½ cup	minced yellow onion	125 ml
½ cup	minced mushroom caps	125 ml
4 cups	chopped spinach leaves	900 ml
½ cup	grated mozzarella cheese	125 ml
1 cup	farmer or ricotta cheese	250 ml
2 cups	rye bread crumbs, coarsely ground	500 ml
½ tsp	ground cumin	½ tsp
¼ tsp	cayenne pepper	¼ tsp
to taste	salt	to taste

1. Preheat oven to 400°F (205°C). Leaving stems on chiles, slit lengthwise and remove seeds and white membrane. Place chiles, cut side up, in lightly oiled baking dish.

2. In a medium skillet heat sherry and olive oil until mixture simmers. Stir in onion and cook over medium-high heat. Keep stirring until onion begins to brown slightly. Add mushrooms and cover; lower heat and cook until mushrooms exude moisture. (Add small amount of water if necessary to prevent mushrooms from sticking.) Remove cover and add spinach. Cover again and cook until spinach is wilted (about 3 minutes).

3. Remove from heat and add remaining ingredients; mix well. Stuff chiles with mushroom mixture.

4. Bake until chiles are softened and cheeses have melted (about 30 minutes). Serve hot.

Serves 6.

POTSTICKERS

These Chinese dumplings are first fried and then steamed, causing the bottoms to stick to the pan slightly.

2 cups	Vegetarian Potsticker Stuffing (see page 38)	500 ml
16	potsticker skins	16
as needed	peanut oil	as needed
¾ cup	water or Vegetarian Stock (see page 16)	175 ml
as needed	dipping sauces (see page 38)	as needed

1. Fill 1 potsticker skin at a time, keeping the remaining skins covered. Place 1 heaping teaspoonful of stuffing across center of skin and lightly moisten edge with a little water. Fold skin in half and pinch together in center, above stuffing. Working on one side of center at a time, pleat the near edge of skin toward center and pinch against the far edge to seal. Continue working outward, making 3 or 4 pleats in all. Repeat on other side of center. Repeat with remaining skins.

2. Heat a heavy skillet over medium-high heat. Add oil to generously coat bottom. When oil is hot, arrange potstickers in pan, pleated sides up, and cook until bottoms begin to brown. Add the water or stock and immediately cover pan. Reduce heat to medium and cook until potstickers have plumped and liquid is nearly evaporated (6–8 minutes).

3. Remove lid and increase heat to medium-high. Cook until liquid boils away and dumplings begin to sizzle. Add oil as necessary for the final browning. Continue cooking until bottoms become crisp and golden brown. Serve with dipping sauces.

Makes 16 potstickers.

Vegetarian Potsticker Stuffing

To prepare the stuffing for the potstickers shown on page 37, purchase pre-fried tofu from a natural food store or Asian market or press firm tofu (see page 63) and fry it in hot oil until puffy and golden brown.

1 clove	garlic	1 clove
¾-inch slice	fresh ginger	1.9-cm slice
¼ cup	cashews, toasted	60 ml
½ cake (3½ oz)	fried tofu	½ cake (100 g)
½ cake (3½ oz)	soft tofu, drained (see page 63)	½ cake (100 g)
2 tsp each	soy sauce and sherry	2 tsp each
1 tsp	Asian sesame oil	1 tsp
1	egg white	1
2 tbl each	minced green onion and diced carrot	2 tbl each
2	dried black mushrooms, soaked and finely diced	2
2 tbl	chopped cilantro (coriander leaves)	2 tbl

1. Using a food processor, add garlic, ginger, and cashews through feed tube while machine is running and process to a fine grind. Add fried and fresh tofu, soy sauce, sherry, and sesame oil; process to a paste.

2. Transfer mixture to a bowl and blend in remaining ingredients.

Makes 1¼ cups (300 ml).

Dipping Sauces

For each tablespoon of soy sauce, add one of these:

- *½ teaspoon grated fresh ginger and a few drops of Asian sesame oil*

- *1 tablespoon each wasabi paste (a pungent condiment) and grated fresh daikon (Japanese white radish)*

- *1 teaspoon grated fresh ginger and ½ teaspoon rice vinegar*

VEGETARIAN SUSHI ROLLS

Sushi rolls can contain a variety of foods, from traditional Japanese ingredients to avocado and other vegetarian fillings (see photo on page 10). Nori and other seaweed products are available at natural food stores and Asian markets.

3 cups	cooked short-grain rice (see page 83)	700 ml
¼ cup	rice vinegar	60 ml
1½ tbl	dry sherry	1½ tbl
3 tbl	honey	3 tbl
2 tsp	salt	2 tsp
6	sheets of toasted nori	6
1	firm cucumber, peeled, seeded, and cut into strips	1
2	carrots, cut into thin strips	2
2	red bell peppers, seeded and cut into thin strips	2
as needed	wasabi-daikon dipping sauce (see page 38)	as needed

1. In a large bowl place cooked rice. In a saucepan over high heat, cook vinegar, sherry, honey, and salt for 5 minutes, stirring occasionally. Pour over rice and stir.

2. Lay out the six sheets of nori and spread an equal amount of rice mixture over each, extending rice almost to edges. Lay a strip of each vegetable along the length of the rice (see Preparing Sushi on pages 40–41).

3. Roll tightly to form a cylinder, then slice each roll into six rounds and place on individual serving dishes. Serve with wasabi-daikon dipping sauce.

Serves 6.

PREPARING SUSHI

The word "sushi" means specially seasoned rice, which is often wrapped with a variety of fillings in toasted nori, a variety of seaweed. The best rice for sushi is short-grain, which is stickier when cooked than long-grain rice. If you must use long-grain rice, cook it with a little extra water. Have all your fillings prepared and organized before you begin rolling the sushi (see recipe on page 39). Serve sushi at room temperature—soon after rolling, before the rice begins to soften the nori.

1. Place rice in a large shallow bowl or baking sheet with sides. Slowly pour marinade over rice while stirring. Fan rice to cool it rapidly. Cover with a damp towel for up to 4 hours while preparing fillings. Do not chill rice in the refrigerator.

2. Using metal tongs, hold nori sheets about 2 inches (5 cm) above a heat source and toast them, passing them back and forth over flame for a few seconds until nori is fragrant and turns dark green.

3. Put bamboo rolling mat on work table with sticks of bamboo parallel to edge of table. Place nori in center of mat. (If you do not have a bamboo rolling mat, cut a piece of aluminum foil about 8 inches or 20 cm square, and place nori in center of foil.) Gently spread sushi rice over nori, leaving ½ inch (1.25 cm) uncovered along all sides.

4. Place small amount of wasabi along length of rice and parallel to bamboo on mat. Wasabi is a fiery condiment; use it sparingly.

5. Place strips of filling along length of sushi rice on top of wasabi and parallel to sticks of bamboo.

6. Lifting bamboo rolling mat from edge nearest to you, start to roll nori and rice over filling ingredients to enclose them. Use roller to press rice onto filling so that rice encloses filling and seals against itself to form a cylinder. Store rolls loosely covered at room temperature until serving time. To serve, slice into 1-inch-thick (2.5-cm) rounds.

Corn Clouds

Fluffy cornmeal batter turns into buttery corn "clouds" you can top with sour cream or yogurt and salsa. When fresh corn is at its peak, serve these dollar-sized pancakes with a selection of cubed avocados, chopped tomatoes, marinated red onion slices, chopped red pepper, or chopped green onion.

1½ cups	unbleached flour	350 ml
½ cup	cornmeal	125 ml
1 tsp	baking powder	1 tsp
6	eggs, separated	6
6 oz	cream cheese	170 g
1½ cups	milk	350 ml
½ cup	unsalted butter, melted	125 ml
¼ cup	minced green onion	60 ml
1 cup	corn kernels cut fresh from cob	250 ml
1 tsp	salt	1 tsp
to taste	hot-pepper sauce	to taste
as needed	oil, for frying	as needed

1. Sift together flour, cornmeal, and baking powder. In electric mixer, cream egg yolks and cream cheese. Add cornmeal mixture, then slowly add milk. Stir in melted butter, green onions, corn kernels, salt, and hot-pepper sauce to taste.

2. In a separate bowl beat egg whites with a pinch of salt until they are stiff but not dry. Fold one third of whites into batter. Then gently fold batter into remaining whites.

3. Lightly grease a nonstick frying pan with oil and heat until oil is fragrant. Drop batter into hot oil by rounded tablespoons and cook until bubbles form and burst on top. Turn cakes over and cook an additional 30 seconds. Transfer cakes to a warm platter and serve.

Makes about 60 dollar-sized cakes.

Vegetarian Egg Rolls

Egg roll wrappers, black mushrooms, and Asian sesame oil are available at Asian markets and many supermarkets. Serve the rolls with any of the dipping sauces on page 38.

3	dried black mushrooms	3
as needed	peanut oil	as needed
3	green onions, minced	3
2 tsp	minced fresh ginger	2 tsp
1 tsp	minced fresh garlic	1 tsp
1/3 lb	white button mushrooms, minced	150 g
1 tsp	Asian sesame oil	1 tsp
1/2 cup	bean sprouts	125 ml
1/4 cup	grated carrots	60 ml
2 tbl	chopped roasted peanuts	2 tbl
12	egg roll wrappers	12

1. Soak the dried mushrooms in hot water to cover for 30 minutes. Drain excess moisture from mushrooms and dice.

2. Heat 2 tablespoons peanut oil in a skillet. Add green onions, ginger, and garlic and cook 3 minutes over moderate heat. Add button mushrooms and cook 2 minutes more. Add black mushrooms and cook 30 seconds. Remove from heat. Stir in sesame oil, bean sprouts, carrots, and peanuts.

3. Fill one wrapper at a time, keeping the remaining wrappers covered to prevent their drying out. Put about 2½ tablespoons filling on the bottom third of each egg roll wrapper. Roll up envelope-fashion, tucking edges over filling. Seal ends by moistening them with a drop of water.

4. In a wok or heavy skillet, heat 4 inches (10 cm) of peanut oil to 375°F (190°C). Fry a few rolls at a time until golden brown on all sides. Drain on paper towels. Serve hot.

Makes 12 egg rolls.

CAULIFLOWER PAKORAS

Spicy East Indian fritters are paired with a refreshing yogurt sauce.

8 tbl	chopped cilantro (coriander leaves)	8 tbl
1 clove	garlic, minced	1 clove
as needed	salt	as needed
1 cup	yogurt	250 ml
1	onion, minced	1
1 clove	garlic, minced	1 clove
as needed	peanut oil, for frying	as needed
4 tsp	minced jalapeño chile	4 tsp
3 sprigs each	parsley and mint, minced	3 sprigs each
1½ cups	unbleached flour	350 ml
1 tbl	baking powder	1 tbl
½ tsp	salt	½ tsp
¼ tsp each	turmeric, ground cumin, and pepper	¼ tsp each
⅛ tsp	cayenne pepper	⅛ tsp
¾ cup	water	175 ml
½ cup	milk	125 ml
3 cups	cauliflower florets, blanched	3 cups

1. In a small bowl combine cilantro, garlic, and a pinch of salt. Stir in yogurt and chill.

2. In a skillet sauté onion and garlic in 1 tablespoon oil over medium heat until soft (about 8 minutes). Stir in chile, parsley, and mint; cook 2–3 minutes more and set aside.

3. In a bowl combine flour, baking powder, ½ teaspoon salt, turmeric, cumin, black pepper, and cayenne pepper. Slowly stir in the water and milk. Let batter rest 30 minutes.

4. Stir onion mixture into batter and add cauliflower. In a deep saucepan heat 3–4 inches (7.5–10 cm) oil to 375°F (190°C). Add a spoonful of batter at a time. Fry 3 minutes, turn over, and fry second side 2 minutes. Remove and drain on paper towels. Serve with yogurt sauce.

Makes about 30 fritters.

MAIN DISHES AND ACCOMPANIMENTS

Vegetarian dishes offer a pleasant change from entrées based on meats, poultry, and fish. Whether you choose easy-to-make Harvest Stir-Fry, elegant Roasted Red Pepper Terrine, or Green Chile Soufflé, the nutritious, satisfying combinations of grains, pasta, beans, and fresh fruits and vegetables in this section will become favorites for both everyday dining and party fare.

TORTA RUSTICA

This peasant-style Italian torta is delicious served hot or at room temperature.

Torta Dough

1 pkg (1 tbl)	active dry yeast	1 pkg (1 tbl)
¼ cup	warm water (110°F or 43°C)	60 ml
1 tbl	honey	1 tbl
½ tsp	salt	½ tsp
2 cups	unbleached flour	500 ml
2	eggs	2
½ cup	butter, softened	125 ml
as needed	olive oil	as needed
¼ cup	olive oil	60 ml
1	unpeeled eggplant, cubed	1
1	onion, finely chopped	1
1 cup	chopped red or green bell pepper	250 ml
2 cloves	garlic, minced	2 cloves
1½ tsp	chopped fresh basil	1½ tsp
½ tsp each	salt and dried oregano	½ tsp each
¼ tsp	freshly ground black pepper	¼ tsp
1 pkg (9 oz)	frozen artichoke hearts	1 pkg (255 g)
1 can (14 ½ oz)	tomatoes, coarsely chopped	1 can (415 g)
3	eggs	3
1 cup	shredded Swiss cheese	250 ml
2 tbl	freshly grated Parmesan cheese	2 tbl

1. To prepare dough, sprinkle yeast over warm water in large bowl of electric mixer; add honey. Let stand until yeast is soft (about 5 minutes). Mix in salt and ½ cup (125 ml) flour. Beat at medium speed until elastic (about 3 minutes). Beat in eggs, one at a time, until smooth. Gradually beat in remaining flour to make a soft dough. Beat in butter, a tablespoon at a time. Place dough in a greased bowl, cover, and let rise in a warm

place until doubled in bulk (1–1½ hours). Stir dough down, cover, and let rest for 10 minutes before shaping.

2. Heat oil in a skillet over medium heat and add eggplant, onion, and bell pepper. Cook until onion is soft. Mix in garlic, basil, salt, oregano, pepper, and artichokes. Add tomatoes and their liquid. Bring mixture to a boil, then reduce heat to a simmer. Cook, stirring occasionally, until eggplant is tender and liquid has evaporated (15–20 minutes). Remove from heat and let cool slightly.

3. Beat two of the eggs in a large bowl. Add vegetable mixture and Swiss cheese; mix and set aside.

4. Shape about two thirds of the dough into a ball on a well-floured surface and roll out to a 14-inch (35-cm) round. Line a well-oiled 8-inch (20-cm) springform pan with dough, pressing it up the sides of the pan.

5. Spread vegetable mixture over dough and fold edge of dough over filling. Roll remaining third of the dough out to a 9-inch (22.5-cm) square; cut into 1-inch-wide (2.5-cm) strips. Weave strips over filling in a lattice pattern, tucking ends of strips around dough lining edge of pan.

6. Preheat oven to 375°F (190°C). Let torta rise until it looks puffy (15–20 minutes). Beat remaining egg with 1 teaspoon water; brush over lattice topping. Sprinkle with Parmesan cheese.

7. Bake until dough is richly browned and filling is set (50 minutes–1 hour). Cool torta in pan on a wire rack for about 10 minutes before removing sides of pan. Cut into wedges and serve warm or at room temperature.

Serves 6 to 8.

Autumn Compote

This harvest of autumn vegetables makes a colorful combination for a speedy supper. Serve over bright Potato Pillows (see recipe and photo on pages 52–53) for a nutritionally complete meal.

1 tbl	corn or olive oil	1 tbl
2	onions, diced	2
3 cloves	garlic, minced	3 cloves
2	red bell peppers, seeded and cut into ½-inch (1.25-cm) pieces	2
2 cups	uncooked corn, cut from the cob	500 ml
2½ cups	sliced green beans	600 ml
2 cups	cooked lima beans	500 ml
½ cup	Vegetarian Stock (see page 16) or water	125 ml
¼ tsp	cayenne pepper	¼ tsp
1 tsp	dried thyme	1 tsp
½ tsp	dried oregano	½ tsp
2 tsp	salt	2 tsp
½ tsp	freshly ground black pepper	½ tsp

1. Heat oil in a large saucepan over medium heat. Add onions and garlic and sauté until soft (about 7–8 minutes).

2. Add red peppers, corn, and green beans, and cook 5 minutes. Add lima beans, the water, cayenne, thyme, oregano, salt, and pepper. Cook 10 minutes and serve hot.

Serves 6.

POTATO PILLOWS

A variation on the traditional German potato pancake, these brightly colored croquettes of shredded vegetables are a good nutritional complement for the lima beans and corn in Autumn Compote (see page 51).

1	potato, peeled	1
1	carrot, scrubbed	1
1	yellow or green zucchini	1
1	onion, minced	1
¾ cup	bread crumbs	175 ml
2	eggs	2
1 tsp	salt	1 tsp
¼ tsp	freshly ground black pepper	¼ tsp
2 tbl	olive oil	2 tbl

1. Shred potato, carrot, and zucchini, using a shredder with large holes.

2. In a large mixing bowl, combine potato, carrot, zucchini, and onion. Stir in bread crumbs, eggs, salt, and pepper. Mix together well and divide mixture into 6 croquettes.

3. Heat oil in a large skillet over medium-high heat. Place croquettes in hot skillet, slightly flattening each to about ⅓ inch (.8 cm) thick. Cook over medium heat until lightly browned (10–12 minutes). Turn and cook the second side for 8–9 minutes. Serve immediately.

Serves 6.

KASHA CROQUETTES WITH MONTEREY-MISO SAUCE

This recipe combines Russian, French, and Pacific Rim influences.

½ cup	kasha (toasted buckwheat groats)	125 ml
1 tsp	salt	1 tsp
2 cups	boiling water	500 ml
½ cup	whole wheat flour or unbleached	125 ml
1	onion, minced	1
as needed	olive oil	as needed
3	green onions, finely chopped	3
½ cup	chopped parsley	125 ml
1	beaten egg	1

Monterey-Miso Sauce

2 cloves	garlic, minced	2 cloves
1 tsp	Asian sesame oil	1 tsp
2 tsp	whole wheat or unbleached flour	2 tsp
1 cup	milk or soy milk	250 ml
3 tsp	miso	3 tsp
2 tbl	hot water	2 tbl
½ tsp	Dijon mustard	½ tsp
¼ cup	grated Monterey jack cheese	60 ml

1. Add kasha and salt to boiling water and cook over medium heat until very soft (15–20 minutes). Let cool, stir in ½ cup flour, and set aside. In a skillet over medium heat sauté onion in 1 tablespoon olive oil until soft (about 2 minutes). Add green onions and parsley, then remove from heat. Mix onion mixture with kasha and stir in egg. Form mixture into 4 croquettes and set aside.

2. To prepare sauce, sauté garlic in sesame oil over medium heat for 1 minute. Add flour and cook, stirring, for 2 more minutes. Slowly add milk, stirring with whisk until sauce thickens. In a

small bowl mix miso with the hot water, stirring until smooth. Add miso, mustard, and cheese to sauce. Set aside and keep warm.

3. Heat a skillet over medium heat and add 1 tablespoon olive oil. Sauté croquettes on both sides until golden (1–2 minutes per side). Serve hot with sauce.

Serves 4.

RED PEPPER TERRINE

Colorful and impressive on its own, this vegetable terrine is also good with a dollop of mayonnaise flavored with a few capers and a bit of tomato paste.

2	unpeeled eggplants	2
as needed	salt	as needed
¼ cup	olive oil	60 ml
1 jar (12 oz)	roasted red bell peppers, drained	1 jar (350 g)
2 tsp	salt	2 tsp
1 cup	fresh basil leaves	250 ml
as needed	parsley sprigs, for garnish	as needed
as needed	sliced black olives, for garnish	as needed

1. Wash and dry eggplants. Cut into ¼-inch-thick (.6-cm) slices and place slices between layers of paper towels on a tray. Sprinkle with salt and let stand for 30 minutes or longer to release excess moisture.

2. Meanwhile, preheat oven to 450°F (230°C). Rinse salt from eggplant slices and pat dry. Lightly brush a baking sheet with 1 tablespoon of the olive oil. Brush both sides of eggplant slices with 3 tablespoons of the olive oil and place on baking sheet. Bake 10 minutes, turn slices over, and bake 10 minutes more. Remove from oven and let cool.

3. Lightly brush a loaf pan with remaining olive oil. Cover bottom of pan with a layer of eggplant slices. Add a layer of roasted red bell peppers; sprinkle with ½ teaspoon salt, then top with 6–8 basil leaves. Layer remaining eggplant, peppers, salt, and basil leaves. Cover the terrine with plastic wrap, place a weight on top of the terrine, and refrigerate 24 hours to set.

4. To unmold, invert terrine on a serving platter. Lift off loaf pan. To serve, cut terrine into 6 thick slices. Garnish with parsley and black olives.

Serves 6.

Eggplant and Chick-Pea Moussaka

Greek cooks traditionally salt eggplant before baking it, to allow the fibers to soften and therefore better absorb the flavors of the other ingredients in the moussaka. The salt can be rinsed off after the initial baking.

1 large	eggplant, sliced thinly	1 large
as needed	salt	as needed
as needed	olive oil	as needed
1	onion, sliced	1
2 cloves	garlic, minced	2 cloves
2	ripe tomatoes, chopped	2
3 tbl	chopped fresh basil	3 tbl
2 tsp	dried oregano	2 tsp
½ cup	white wine	125 ml
1 cup	cooked chick-peas	250 ml
2	eggs, beaten lightly	2
2 tbl	freshly grated Parmesan cheese	2 tbl

1. Preheat oven to 300°F. Place eggplant slices on a large baking tray and lightly sprinkle with salt. Bake until easily pierced with a fork (about 10 to 15 minutes).

2. While eggplant is baking, heat 1 tablespoon olive oil in a skillet and sauté onion until soft, then add garlic, tomatoes, basil, oregano, and wine. Continue to cook until tomatoes soften (about 10 minutes).

3. Rinse salt from eggplant, if desired. Place eggplant slices in a lightly oiled 9- by 12-inch baking dish. Raise temperature of oven to 350°F.

4. Spread chick-peas over eggplant; top with beaten eggs. Spoon tomato mixture over eggs. Sprinkle with cheese and bake for 45 minutes. Serve hot.

Serves 4.

SANDWICH STYLINGS

A bit of imagination improves almost any sandwich. Try replacing the standard lettuce leaf with salad sprouts, cabbage, shredded carrot or chopped celery, sliced jicama, or lightly steamed kale or other leafy greens; or substituting rolls, baguettes, focaccia, pita bread, or tortillas for sliced sandwich bread. Many sandwich spreads and nut butter combinations go well with crudités (raw vegetables), chips, crackers, or bread sticks. Try some of the following suggestions for lunch or, for a change of pace, for breakfast.

Each of the following sandwich recipes serves 4:

Swiss Garden Sauté *Sauté in 1 tablespoon olive oil 1 cup (250 ml) sliced fresh mushrooms and ¼ cup (60 ml) each diced bell pepper, onion, and zucchini just until softened. Divide mixture among 4 slices whole grain toast. Top each with 1 slice Swiss cheese and broil until cheese melts.*

Hummus Salad *In a blender, purée 1½ cups (350 ml) canned chick-peas, 2 cloves of garlic, ½ teaspoon soy sauce or tamari, ¼ cup (60 ml) lemon juice, and ⅓ cup (85 ml) tahini (sesame butter). Cut 2 pita breads into halves to make 4 pockets. Spoon a fourth of the hummus mixture into each of the pockets and add chopped fresh tomatoes, bell peppers, and a spoonful of yogurt.*

Provençale *Drain and chop ¼ cup sun-dried tomatoes packed in oil. Add 4 ounces crumbled goat cheese, and ⅛ teaspoon dried thyme. Blend with fork and spread on toasted French bread. Top with minced parsley.*

California Melt *Divide 1 sliced avocado, 1 cup (250 ml) sliced fresh mushrooms, ⅓ cup (85 ml) sliced toasted almonds, and 1 thinly sliced tomato among 4 slices whole grain toast. Top each with a slice of provolone or Cheddar cheese and broil until cheese melts.*

Mauna Loa Melt Top each of 4 slices of buttered raisin toast with salad sprouts, 2 fresh or canned pineapple rings, and 1 slice mozzarella cheese. Broil until cheese melts.

Santa Fe Melt Sauté in 1 tablespoon olive oil $^1/_4$ cup (60 ml) each diced bell pepper and onion. Add $1^1/_2$ cups (350 ml) cooked and drained pinto beans, mashing beans with a fork as mixture heats. Add salsa to taste and divide mixture among 4 corn or flour tortillas or whole grain toast. Top with shredded Monterey jack cheese and broil until cheese melts.

Fresh nut butters are easy to prepare in a blender or food processor. Use almonds, cashews, peanuts, pecans, walnuts or a combination, toasted or untoasted, salted or unsalted. Depending on the type of nuts you use, add a little canola, walnut, or olive oil to keep the mixture smooth during processing. After you've made the nut butter, try one of the following combinations on whole grain bread, toast, crackers, or pieces of fresh vegetable or fruit. Adjust the proportions of nut butter and other ingredients in the following combinations to suit your taste:

Tropical Nectar Nut butter, sliced mango or papaya sprinkled with lime juice, and honey to taste.

Banana-Coconut Nut butter, thinly sliced bananas sprinkled with lemon juice, and coconut shreds.

Apple Butter-Pear Nut butter, spiced apple butter, and finely chopped pear.

Applesauce-Raisin Nut butter, applesauce, raisins.

Apple-Cabbage Nut butter, finely chopped apple, and shredded red or green cabbage.

Pecan Burgers

These nut-and-vegetable burgers will satisfy vegetarians and hamburger lovers alike. Be sure the pecans are fresh; you can easily grind them yourself in a blender or food processor. Try serving these burgers on Kaiser rolls or sourdough toast garnished with tomato slices, red onion rings, and lettuce. You can mix and shape the burgers and then refrigerate them for up to a day before cooking them. If you prefer, you can also broil these burgers 2–3 minutes on each side.

1 cup	ground pecans or pecan meal	250 ml
½ cup	wheat germ	125 ml
½ cup	cooked oatmeal	125 ml
½	onion, grated	½
1	carrot, grated	1
1 tbl	Asian sesame oil	1 tbl
1 tsp	soy sauce or tamari	1 tsp
1	egg, lightly beaten (optional)	1
as needed	unbleached or whole wheat flour	as needed
as needed	oil, for frying	as needed

1. In a large bowl mix all ingredients. The egg adds protein and helps bind the mixture together, but is not essential. If the egg is used, you may need to add a teaspoon or so of flour to keep the mixture from being too moist to form into burgers. Shape the mixture into 4 burgers and set aside or refrigerate for up to 24 hours.

2. Heat skillet over medium heat and add a small amount of oil. When oil is fragrant, add burgers and sauté lightly on both sides until browned (about 3–4 minutes per side). Serve hot.

Makes 4 burgers.

ABOUT TOFU

Highly versatile, inexpensive, and nutritious, tofu (soybean curd) is fast becoming almost as commonplace in American supermarkets as it is in Asian markets.

With a color and texture much like that of soft cheese, tofu is made by a process similar to that used for making its dairy counterpart. Dried soybeans are soaked and ground, then blended with water, and strained and heated. A curdling agent is added, causing the mixture to separate into cheeselike solids (curds) surrounded by liquid (whey). The solids are poured into a press, and after about 30 minutes, the tofu is firm enough to be cut into blocks or cakes.

Fresh tofu is highly perishable but keeps well up to 10 days, refrigerated and stored in fresh water in a sealed package or closed container. The water should be replaced every two days. Tofu is also available in airtight cartons that require no refrigeration until the package is opened. Fresh tofu can be frozen for up to 1 month, although freezing changes its texture. After thawing, it should be squeezed to remove excess water and then crumbled. The texture of thawed tofu resembles that of ground beef or turkey, making it ideal for use in vegetarian chili, lasagne, and other dishes traditionally made with meat.

Two varieties of fresh tofu are widely available: soft (silken)—best for blending into sauces, salad dressings, cream soups, casseroles, and creamy desserts; and firm (nigari)—best for stir-frying, since it holds its shape well. Pressing tofu before sautéing, stir-frying or baking it removes excess moisture, enabling the tofu to hold its shape. To press firm tofu, slice it into 1/2-inch (1.25-cm) slices and place between several layers of clean kitchen towels. Place a heavy chopping board or heavy pot filled with water on top of the towels and leave weight in place for 15–45 minutes. Then remove tofu and proceed with the recipe.

SWEET-AND-SOUR TOFU-PEPPER SAUTÉ

Crunchy, brightly colored bell peppers complement protein-rich tofu in this spicy dish. The vegetables and tofu can be marinated ahead of time for added flavor, and you can reheat any leftovers for lunch the next day. Arrowroot powder, available at natural food stores and specialty food stores, thickens at a lower temperature than flour or cornstarch and is ideal for quick-cooking dishes like this one.

1 cup	thinly sliced red bell pepper	250 ml
½ cup	thinly sliced green bell pepper	125 ml
⅓ cup	thinly sliced yellow bell pepper	85 ml
2 tsp	olive oil	2 tsp
1 tbl	arrowroot powder	1 tbl
½ cup	rice vinegar	125 ml
½ cup	pineapple juice	125 ml
½ cup	fresh lemon juice	125 ml
⅓ cup	honey	85 ml
½ tsp	salt	½ tsp
½ tsp	grated fresh ginger	½ tsp
2 cakes (7 oz each)	firm tofu, sliced and pressed (see page 63)	2 cakes (200 g each)
2 tbl	soy sauce or tamari	2 tbl
as needed	cayenne pepper	as needed

1. In a wok over medium-high heat, toss bell peppers in oil until lightly cooked (about 5 minutes).

2. In a large bowl combine arrowroot, vinegar, pineapple juice, lemon juice, honey, salt, and ginger. Pour over peppers and cook at medium heat, stirring, just until mixture thickens slightly.

3. Add tofu to wok, cover, and steam 3 minutes. Add soy sauce and cayenne to taste. Toss well and serve.

Serves 6.

SUMMER STIR-FRY MÉLANGE

Stir-frying is a natural for busy cooks. Be sure to have the tofu and all of the vegetables prepared before you begin cooking—this dish comes together quickly when everything is organized ahead of time. Rice (see page 83) is a satisfying accompaniment to this easy dish.

1 cake (7 oz)	firm tofu, sliced and pressed (see page 63)	1 cake (200 g)
3 tbl	olive oil	3 tbl
1–3 cloves	garlic, minced	1–3 cloves
2 tsp	grated fresh ginger	2 tsp
1	red onion, sliced	1
2	green or red bell peppers, seeded and diced	2
1½ cups	sliced green beans	350 ml
1	carrot, coarsely grated	1
¾ lb	mushrooms, sliced	350 g
1 bunch	Swiss chard or bok choy, chopped	1 bunch
1	zucchini, sliced	1
½ tsp	dried thyme	½ tsp
2 tbl	minced parsley	2 tbl
1 tsp	fresh lemon juice	1 tsp
2–3 tbl	soy sauce or tamari	2–3 tbl

1. Cube pressed tofu and set aside. In a large wok or frying pan, heat oil, garlic, and ginger.

2. Add onion, bell peppers, beans, and carrot. Stir-fry over high heat 4 minutes.

3. Add mushrooms, chard, zucchini, herbs, and tofu. Pour lemon juice and soy sauce over vegetables and stir-fry just until tender but still crisp (4–5 minutes). Serve at once.

Serves 4.

Thai Eggplant in Chile Marinade

Marinated in dried chiles and miso, this Thai specialty can be served warm or at room temperature. Double the amount of dried red chiles for a hotter sensation. The Asian sesame oil and miso are available in natural food stores and Asian markets.

12	small Japanese eggplants	12
½ tsp	salt	½ tsp
2	green onions, minced	2
2 cloves	garlic, minced	2 cloves
1 tsp	cilantro (coriander leaves), minced	1 tsp
1 tsp	Asian sesame oil	1 tsp
3 tbl	peanut butter	3 tbl
2 tbl	rice vinegar	2 tbl
5 tbl	water	5 tbl
½ tsp	ground dried red chiles	½ tsp
2 tbl	miso	2 tbl

1. Preheat oven to 350°F (175°C). Slice eggplants in half lengthwise and sprinkle with salt. Place upside down on paper towels on a tray and let stand for 20 minutes to release excess moisture. Rinse salt from eggplants and pat dry. Place eggplants, cut side down, on a baking sheet and bake for 25 minutes. Set aside.

2. In a medium bowl, combine green onions, garlic, cilantro, sesame oil, peanut butter, rice vinegar, the water, red chiles, and miso. Stir to mix thoroughly.

3. Slice baked eggplants into ½-inch-thick (1.25-cm) strips and toss with chile mixture. Serve warm or at room temperature.

Serves 6.

HARVEST STIR-FRY

Nothing displays the fresh tastes of autumn as simply as a stir-fry of fresh produce (shown with Thai Eggplant in the photo on page 69). Look for sesame seed and Asian sesame oil in Asian markets or natural food stores.

2 tbl	black or white sesame seed	2 tbl
½ lb	fresh shiitake or button mushrooms	225 g
1	red bell pepper	1
1 bunch	broccoli	1 bunch
5	baby bok choy, quartered	5
2 cloves	garlic, peeled	2 cloves
1-inch cube	fresh ginger	2.5-cm cube
1 tbl	olive oil	1 tbl
2 tbl	water	2 tbl
1	onion	1
2 tbl	soy sauce or tamari	2 tbl
1 tsp	Asian sesame oil	1 tsp

1. In a dry skillet over medium heat toast the sesame seed until fragrant. Do not allow it to scorch. Set aside. Slice mushrooms and pepper into pieces about ½ inch (1.25 cm) thick. Separate the broccoli florets and slice the stems thinly. Cut bok choy in quarters lengthwise. Mince garlic and ginger.

2. In a wok or large skillet heat olive oil over medium-high heat. Add garlic and ginger to hot oil, stirring constantly, and cook 1 minute. Stir in broccoli. Add the water and cook for 3 minutes.

3. Add onion and cook, stirring constantly, 3 minutes. Add bok choy and cook for 2 minutes, stirring constantly. Stir in pepper and mushrooms and cook for 2 minutes longer. Stir in soy sauce and sesame oil. Sprinkle with toasted sesame seed and serve immediately.

Serves 6.

WOK AND STIR-FRY TECHNIQUES

Main dishes stir-fried in a wok cook in minutes, and the ingredients can be prepared up to four hours before cooking. Stir-fry cooking is always done rapidly, over medium-high or high heat, a method that preserves the color, texture, flavor, and nutritional value of the ingredients. Because of the speed of the cooking process, be sure to have all the tools you will need—wok, utensils, and serving dish—and all the ingredients prepared for cooking and close at hand before you turn on the heat. The flavor of Asian sesame oil or peanut oil complements most stir-fried dishes. Although olive oil adds a pleasing flavor, it has a lower smoking point than most other oils and is best used for stir-frying blanched vegetables and other ingredients that don't require prolonged cooking over high heat.

1. Begin by heating the wok and adding the oil in a thin stream around the outside of the wok. Rotate the wok to distribute the oil evenly over the surface.

2. When ripples form on the surface of the oil, add the first ingredient (the one that takes the longest time to cook). Toss the food in the hot oil until well coated. As the food cooks, add the ingredients in the order given in the recipe. When the ingredients are cooked to taste but still bright in color, transfer the food to a serving dish and serve at once.

MIXED VEGETABLES WITH ALMONDS

A colorful assortment of fresh vegetables with crunchy almonds fits equally well into an Eastern or Western menu.

2 cups	broccoli florets	500 ml
as needed	lightly salted boiling water	as needed
1 tsp	cornstarch	1 tsp
2 tbl each	soy sauce and dry sherry	2 tbl each
3 tbl	Asian sesame oil	3 tbl
¼ cup	whole blanched almonds	60 ml
1 tsp	minced fresh ginger	1 tsp
4	green onions, coarsely chopped	4
1	red or green bell pepper, seeded and cut into 1-inch (2.5-cm) squares	1
1 cup	sliced celery	250 ml
8–12 ears	canned baby corn, drained	8–12 ears
½ cup	sliced fresh shiitake or button mushrooms	125 ml

1. Blanch broccoli florets in lightly salted boiling water for 30 seconds. Transfer to a bowl of ice water to stop cooking. Remove from ice water after 30 seconds, drain, and set aside.

2. Dissolve cornstarch in mixture of soy sauce and sherry, and set aside.

3. Heat wok over medium heat and add oil. Add almonds and cook, stirring constantly, until they begin to brown. Remove and drain on paper towels.

4. Remove all but 1 tablespoon oil from wok and increase heat to medium-high. Add ginger and cook a few seconds until fragrant. Add green onions, bell pepper, celery, and baby corn. Cook 1 minute, stirring constantly. Add broccoli to wok along with mushrooms and almonds. Stir-fry just until mushrooms soften. Stir cornstarch mixture and add to wok. Stir and cook until sauce thickens and becomes glossy. Transfer to a warm serving platter and serve at once.

Serves 4.

BROCCOLI-MUSHROOM STIR-FRY
WITH LINGUINE

A colorful combination of quick-cooking ingredients makes this recipe easy to put together; the actual cooking takes less than 10 minutes. Precut the broccoli stalks, slice the mushrooms and water chestnuts, and cook the linguine pasta ahead of time; store these ingredients in the refrigerator. Be sure not to overcook the broccoli; its crispness and bright green color are essential to the success of this dish. Look for the Asian sesame oil in Asian markets or natural food stores.

2 tsp	minced garlic	2 tsp
2 tsp	Asian sesame oil	2 tsp
1 cup	sliced shiitake or domestic mushrooms	250 ml
4 cups	broccoli florets	900 ml
½ cup	sliced water chestnuts, drained	125 ml
4 cups	cooked and drained linguine	900 ml
2 tbl	soy sauce or tamari	2 tbl
¼ cup	minced green onions	60 ml

1. In a wok or large skillet over medium-high heat, sauté garlic in sesame oil for 1 minute. Add mushrooms and cook until they exude moisture (about 2–3 minutes).

2. Add broccoli and water chestnuts and stir-fry for about 3 minutes. Add linguine, soy sauce, and green onions. Toss together well. Cover and steam for 2 minutes, then serve at once.

Serves 6.

SPAGHETTI WITH VEGETABLE RIBBONS

Whole wheat spaghetti combined with thin ribbons of carrot and green and yellow zucchini makes for a colorful pasta dish. You can substitute your favorite pasta for the whole wheat variety if you prefer.

3	carrots, scrubbed	3
3	green zucchini	3
3	yellow zucchini	3
1 tbl	olive oil	1 tbl
1 tbl	butter	1 tbl
2 cloves	garlic, minced	2 cloves
½ lb	whole wheat spaghetti, cooked and drained	225 g
1½ cups	tightly packed fresh basil, minced	350 ml
¾ cup	minced parsley	175 ml
½ cup	minced fresh chives	125 ml
2 tbl	minced fresh marjoram	2 tbl
1½ tsp	salt	1½ tsp
½ cup	freshly grated Parmesan cheese	125 ml

1. Grate or cut carrots and green and yellow zucchini into long, thin strips (about ⅛ inch or .3 cm thick) to resemble spaghetti.

2. In a Dutch oven or large skillet, heat oil and butter over low heat. Add garlic and carrots. Sauté for 5–7 minutes. Add whole wheat spaghetti, green and yellow zucchini, basil, parsley, chives, marjoram, and salt. Stir to combine and cook for 4–5 minutes.

3. Remove from heat and place in a shallow serving bowl. Sprinkle with Parmesan cheese. Toss to combine and serve immediately.

Serves 6 to 8.

LASAGNE CON SPINACI

If you're looking for a lasagne recipe that's low on fat, high on flavor, and simple to make, try this one.

1 can (28 oz)	Italian-style tomatoes, crushed	1 can (800 g)
1 clove	garlic, minced	1 clove
½ tsp each	dried thyme and oregano	½ tsp each
1 lb	lasagne	450 g
2 cups	sliced onions	500 ml
2 cups	sliced mushrooms	500 ml
1 cup	white wine	250 ml
2 cups	chopped spinach leaves	500 ml
1 tsp	salt	1 tsp
1 cup	firm tofu, pressed (see page 63)	250 ml
1 cup	part-skim ricotta cheese	250 ml
as needed	olive oil	as needed
2 tbl	freshly grated Parmesan cheese	2 tbl
¼ cup	bread crumbs	60 ml

1. In a saucepan over medium heat mix tomatoes, garlic, and herbs. Bring to a boil, reduce heat, and simmer, uncovered, 10–15 minutes. Set aside.

2. Cook and drain pasta and set aside.

3. Cook onions and mushrooms in white wine over medium heat until soft (about 10 minutes). Add spinach and salt and cook, covered, for 1 minute. Remove from heat. Crumble pressed tofu, mix with ricotta, and stir into vegetable mixture.

4. Preheat oven to 375°F (190°C). Lightly oil a large baking dish. Assemble lasagne by alternating layers of spinach mixture, tomato mixture, and lasagne, ending with lasagne on top. Sprinkle Parmesan cheese and bread crumbs over top of lasagne. Drizzle a little olive oil over top, if desired. Bake until bubbly (about 30 minutes). Allow to stand 5 minutes before serving.

Serves 6 to 8.

CURRIED POLENTA

In this cross-cultural version of a northern Italian classic, baked polenta is topped with sautéed vegetables in a spicy curry sauce.

as needed	olive oil	as needed
1 cup	sliced onion	250 ml
½ cup	julienned carrots	125 ml
1 tsp	minced garlic	1 tsp
3 tbl	chopped parsley	3 tbl
½ tsp	ground cumin	½ tsp
1 tsp	ground coriander	1 tsp
2 tsp	curry powder	2 tsp
¼ cup	apple juice	60 ml
½ tsp	cayenne pepper	½ tsp
¾ cup	polenta	175 ml
½ cup	cold water	125 ml
½ tsp	salt	½ tsp
2 cups	boiling water	500 ml
1 cup	grated Monterey jack cheese	250 ml

1. In a large skillet over medium-high heat, heat 1 teaspoon oil and sauté onion for 5 minutes, stirring frequently. Add carrots, garlic, and parsley, and sauté 5 more minutes. Add cumin, coriander, curry powder, apple juice, and cayenne. Cover, reduce heat to very low, and simmer while polenta cooks.

2. Preheat oven to 350°F (175°C). In a bowl mix polenta, the cold water, and salt. Stir the polenta mixture into the boiling water, whisking until smooth. Cook over medium heat, whisking frequently, until thick (5–10 minutes). Stir in cheese.

3. Spoon polenta into a lightly oiled shallow baking dish and bake 20 minutes. To serve, slice polenta into wedges and top with a spoonful of curried vegetables. Serve immediately.

Serves 6.

GREEN CHILE SOUFFLÉ

This quick and easy soufflé is equally good as breakfast, brunch, or late-night supper.

1 tsp	butter	1 tsp
4	eggs	4
1 can (27 oz)	green chiles, drained	1 can (770 g)
1	fresh jalapeño chile, seeded and chopped	1
1 tsp	salt	1 tsp
¼ cup	unbleached flour	60 ml
3 cups	cooked brown rice (see page 83)	700 ml
1½ cups	grated Monterey jack cheese	350 ml

1. Lightly butter a shallow baking dish. Preheat oven to 400°F (205°C).

2. Separate egg yolks from egg whites. Place yolks, one fourth of the canned chiles, jalapeño chile, salt, and flour into a blender or food processor. Purée until smooth. Place egg whites in a bowl and beat until soft peaks form. Stir a third of the egg whites into chile-egg mixture and fold in remaining egg whites.

3. Place another fourth of the canned chiles in bottom of prepared baking dish. Cover with one third of the rice, one third of the cheese, and one third of the chile-egg mixture. Layer with another fourth of the canned chiles, half of the remaining rice, half of the remaining cheese, and half of the remaining chile-egg mixture. Top with the remaining chiles and the remaining rice, cheese, and chile-egg mixture.

4. Bake until top is golden brown (30–35 minutes). Serve hot.

Serves 8.

COOKING RICE

If there's a foolproof technique for cooking rice, it's the absorption method, which works for both white and brown rice and is faster than steaming:

1. Measure the rice, allowing ⅓–⅔ cup (85–150 ml) uncooked rice per serving, into a large bowl or pot. Add cold water to cover the rice by several inches and swirl the water vigorously until it turns cloudy. Drain rice through a strainer. Repeat the swirling and straining procedure until water is clear, 3–5 times in all. Drain rice thoroughly and transfer to cooking pot.

2. Measure the water, using the proper ratio of water for the type of rice to be cooked.

- For long-grain use 2 cups (500 ml) water for the first cup (250 ml) of rice and 1 cup (250 ml) of water for each additional cup (250 ml).

- For medium- and short-grain use 1½ cups (350 ml) water for the first cup (250 ml) of rice and 1 cup (250 ml) of water for each additional cup (250 ml).

3. Bring water to a boil, cover, reduce heat, and simmer until water is absorbed. Short- or medium-grain white rice will take about 15 minutes; short- or medium-grain brown will take 25–30 minutes. Long-grain rice (white or brown) cooks more quickly than short- or medium-grain, so time it accordingly. Lift the cover just long enough to check whether the rice has absorbed the water, then quickly replace the cover. When all the water is absorbed, turn off the heat and let the rice stand, covered, 10 minutes longer. Fluff with a fork or chopsticks before serving.

LENTIL RAGOÛT PRINTANIER

When spring rains make you long for a vegetarian stew with substance, this combination of lentils and seasonal produce cannot be surpassed. The green lentils imported from France hold their shape a little better than other varieties, but you can use any type of lentil.

1 tbl	olive oil	1 tbl
2	onions, diced	2
4 cloves	garlic, minced	4 cloves
2 cups	lentils	500 ml
4 cups	Vegetarian Stock (see page 16) or water	900 ml
½ cup	chopped fresh parsley	125 ml
1 tsp	dried oregano	1 tsp
1 tsp	dried thyme	1 tsp
1 tsp	salt	1 tsp
½ tsp	freshly ground black pepper	½ tsp
12	baby turnips	12
12	small carrots, coarsely chopped	12
6	green onions, coarsely chopped	6
1½ lb	fresh peas, shelled	680 g

1. In a large saucepan over medium heat, heat oil and cook onion and garlic together for 7–8 minutes.

2. Wash lentils. Sort and discard broken pieces. Add lentils, stock, parsley, oregano, thyme, salt, and pepper to saucepan. Simmer for 20 minutes.

3. Cut turnips in half or quarters. Add turnips and carrots to saucepan and cook for 10 minutes. Add green onions and peas, and cook for 5 minutes more. Serve hot.

Serves 6.

Herbed Buckwheat Crêpes

A savory vegetable mixture fills these delicate crêpes.

2 tbl	butter	2 tbl
2 cloves	garlic, minced	2 cloves
5	leeks, finely chopped	5
4	green onions, chopped	4
¼ lb	porcini or button mushrooms, quartered	115 g
4 cups	coarsely chopped spinach leaves	900 ml
¼ cup	yogurt	60 ml
to taste	salt and white pepper	to taste

Buckwheat-Dill Crêpes

¾ cup	water	175 ml
½ cup	milk	125 ml
2	eggs	2
as needed	olive oil	as needed
¼ cup	buckwheat flour	60 ml
¾ cup	unbleached flour	175 ml
1 tbl	dried dill	1 tbl
¼ tsp	salt	¼ tsp

1. In a skillet over medium heat melt butter; add garlic and leeks and cook 10 minutes. Add onions, mushrooms, and spinach; cook 10 more minutes. Stir in yogurt, salt, and pepper and set aside.

2. To prepare crêpes, combine all ingredients and whisk until smooth. Let rest 30 minutes. Heat a crêpe pan over medium heat and brush with oil. Drizzle 2 tablespoons batter into pan, turning pan to coat evenly. Cook for about 1 minute, turn and cook for 30 seconds more. Remove to a plate and repeat with remaining batter.

3. Preheat oven to 350°F (175°C). Spread 1 tablespoon of filling on each crêpe, fold into quarters, and place in dish. Cover and bake 20 minutes. Remove cover and bake 5 minutes more. Serve at once.

Serves 6.

COUSCOUS WITH CURRIED MUSHROOMS

Platters of sweet, nutty couscous are a staple in Middle Eastern restaurants and households. This simple curried variation can be made ahead and reheated before serving.

½ cup	sliced onion	125 ml
2 tsp	minced garlic	2 tsp
1 tsp	olive oil	1 tsp
1 cup	sliced button mushrooms	250 ml
½ cup	grated carrots	125 ml
1 tsp	curry powder	1 tsp
¼ tsp	turmeric	¼ tsp
½ tsp	ground coriander	½ tsp
2 tsp	cinnamon	2 tsp
½ cup	raisins	125 ml
3 cups	Vegetarian Stock (see page 16)	700 ml
2 tbl	soy sauce or tamari	2 tbl
½ cup	chopped parsley	125 ml
2 cups	uncooked couscous	500 ml

1. In a large skillet over medium-high heat, sauté onions and garlic in oil for 2 minutes, stirring frequently. Add mushrooms and carrots and cook for 5 minutes.

2. Add curry powder, turmeric, coriander, cinnamon, and raisins, and cook for 3 minutes more. Add stock and bring to a boil.

3. Stir in soy sauce, parsley, and couscous. Cover pan and remove from heat. Let stand until liquid has been absorbed (about 15 minutes). Fluff couscous with a fork. Serve hot.

Serves 4.

SPECIAL-OCCASION DESSERTS

With fresh fruits and vegetables providing the color in the fabric of vegetarian cooking, these ingredients are natural components for the perfect ending to a fine vegetarian meal. Made from a luscious blend of seasonal produce and other nutritious ingredients, the four desserts in this section are ideal for any special occasion, from a dinner party to a celebratory snack.

MAPLE-CASHEW CHEESECAKE

Arrowroot powder replaces eggs as the thickener for this cheesecake.

2½ cups	finely crushed graham cracker crumbs	600 ml
1 tsp	cinnamon	1 tsp
¼ cup	sugar or date sugar	60 ml
¼ cup	canola or corn oil	60 ml
1 cup	nonfat or soy milk	250 ml
½ cup	ground cashews	125 ml
½ cup	water	125 ml
⅓ cup	arrowroot powder	85 ml
3 tbl	pure vanilla extract	3 tbl
⅔ cup	maple syrup	150 ml
⅔ cup	carob or cocoa powder	150 ml
8 oz	low-fat cream cheese	225 g
3 cups	nonfat yogurt or low-fat sour cream	700 ml
3 tbl each	unsalted butter and honey	3 tbl each
2 tbl	chopped almonds	2 tbl

1. Preheat oven to 300°F (150°C). In a bowl combine graham cracker crumbs, cinnamon, sugar, oil, and milk. Press mixture into sides and bottom of a 9-inch (22.5-cm) springform pan.

2. In a blender purée cashews and the water. Add ¼ cup (60 ml) of the arrowroot, 1 tablespoon of the vanilla, half the maple syrup, ⅓ cup (85 ml) of carob or cocoa powder, and cream cheese and blend until very smooth. Pour into prepared crust and bake 30 minutes, then cool 15 minutes in pan.

3. In blender mix yogurt with remaining maple syrup and remaining vanilla. Pour over baked cheesecake and return it to oven. Bake 10 minutes more, then cool 10 minutes in pan.

4. In blender or food processor, purée butter, honey, and remaining milk, carob or cocoa powder, and arrowroot. Pour over baked cheesecake and sprinkle with chopped almonds. Chill for 6 hours before serving.

Makes 1 nine-inch (22.5-cm) cheesecake.

CRANBERRY TURNOVERS WITH MAPLE GLAZE

Turnovers make an easy dessert for brunch.

1 pkg (1 tbl)	active dry yeast	1 pkg (1 tbl)
1 cup	warm milk (105°F or 41°C)	250 ml
3 tbl	honey	3 tbl
3 cups	unbleached pastry flour	700 ml
as needed	salt and corn oil	as needed
¾ cup	fresh cranberries	175 ml
2 cups	cored, peeled, and sliced green apples	500 ml
½ cup	water	125 ml
¼ cup	dried currants	60 ml
1 cup	maple syrup	250 ml
3 tbl	arrowroot powder	3 tbl
1 tbl each	fresh lemon juice and lemon zest	1 tbl each
½ tsp	cinnamon	½ tsp

1. In a bowl combine yeast, milk, and honey and let stand for 5 minutes. Stir in 1½ cups (350 ml) of the flour and let rise for 15 minutes. Add remaining flour, a pinch of salt, and 3 tablespoons oil to form a dough. Knead for 5 minutes, then cover dough and let rise for 45 minutes.

2. In a covered saucepan over medium heat, simmer cranberries, apples, the water, and currants until berries pop. In a bowl mix ⅔ cup (150 ml) of the maple syrup, arrowroot, lemon juice, zest, and cinnamon; stir into cranberry mixture. Cook, stirring constantly, until thick. Remove from heat and let cool.

3. Preheat oven to 375°F (190°C. Divide dough into 8 balls and roll out into 5-inch (12.5-cm) rounds. Spoon cranberry filling into center of each round. Dampen edges of rounds with water and fold to form a turnover, pressing to seal.

4. Boil remaining maple syrup for 3 minutes. Remove from heat and brush turnovers with syrup. Place turnovers on oiled baking sheet and bake about 20 minutes. Cool slightly before serving.

Makes 8 turnovers.

POIVRE AU ZINFANDEL

Heating wine to 170°F (77°C) evaporates the alcohol while the aroma and flavor remain. Make these wine-poached pears up to one week ahead of time and serve them chilled. Save the poaching liquid for up to four months in the refrigerator and use it again and again.

2 tbl	lemon juice	2 tbl
2 cups	Zinfandel or Burgundy wine	500 ml
1 tsp	honey	1 tsp
2 tsp	cinnamon	2 tsp
1 cup	orange juice	250 ml
6 large	pears, slightly underripe	6 large
as needed	fresh mint leaves, for garnish	as needed

1. In a deep saucepan mix all ingredients except pears and mint leaves.

2. Core whole pears from the bottom, using a melon baller or corer and leaving stems intact. Peel the pears and set aside.

3. Bring the mixture in the saucepan to a boil, add pears, and simmer until they become deep red in color and soft but still hold their shape (about 35 minutes). Drain pears and chill, reserving poaching liquid for another use. Garnish pears with mint leaves and serve.

Serves 6.

ORANGE-PUMPKIN SPICE CUSTARD

Scented with spices, this easy custard dessert is a fine treat for a holiday party, especially since it takes a relatively short time to prepare.

as needed	corn oil	as needed
1 cup	nonfat or soy milk	250 ml
1 tbl	arrowroot powder	1 tbl
2 tbl	molasses	2 tbl
1 cup	canned or cooked pumpkin purée	250 ml
1 tbl	cinnamon	1 tbl
½ tsp	ground cloves	½ tsp
1 tsp	ground cardamom	1 tsp
2 tsp	grated fresh ginger	2 tsp
1 tsp	freshly grated nutmeg	1 tsp
½ cup	maple syrup	125 ml
2 tbl	grated orange zest	2 tbl
¼ cup	freshly squeezed orange juice	60 ml
2	eggs	2
as needed	nonfat yogurt, for garnish	as needed

1. Preheat oven to 350°F (175°C). Lightly oil 8 custard cups.

2. In a large bowl combine milk, arrowroot, and molasses, and whisk until well blended. Add pumpkin, cinnamon, cloves, cardamom, ginger, nutmeg, maple syrup, orange zest, and orange juice.

3. Separate eggs. Beat yolks and add to pumpkin mixture. In a small bowl beat egg whites until stiff peaks form. Fold into pumpkin mixture.

4. Pour mixture into prepared custard cups. Place in a shallow baking pan. Carefully add hot water until level reaches halfway up the sides of pan. Bake custard until just firm (about 40 minutes). Let cool slightly and serve at once, garnished with yogurt.

Serves 8.

Index